PROPERTY OF

D1383381

WEST VIRGINIA

A Turner Educational Services, Inc. book. Based on the Portrait of America television series created by R.E. (Ted) Turner.

Library of Congress Number: 87-26483

Library of Congress Cataloging in Publication Data

Thompson, Kathleen.
West Virginia.

(Portrait of America)
"A Turner book."
Summary: Discusses the history, economy, culture, and future of West Virginia. Also includes a state chronology, pertinent statistics, and maps.
1. West Virginia—Juvenile literature. [1. West Virginia]
I. Title. II. Series: Thompson, Kathleen.
Portrait of America.
F241.3.T48 1987 975.4—dc19 87-26483

ISBN 0-8174-476-1 hardcover library binding

ISBN 0-8114-6816-X softcover binding

Cover Photo: National Park Service

4 5 6 7 8 9 0 96 95 94 93 92 91

★ ★ ★ ★ ★

Portrait of AMERICA

WEST VIRGINIA

Kathleen Thompson

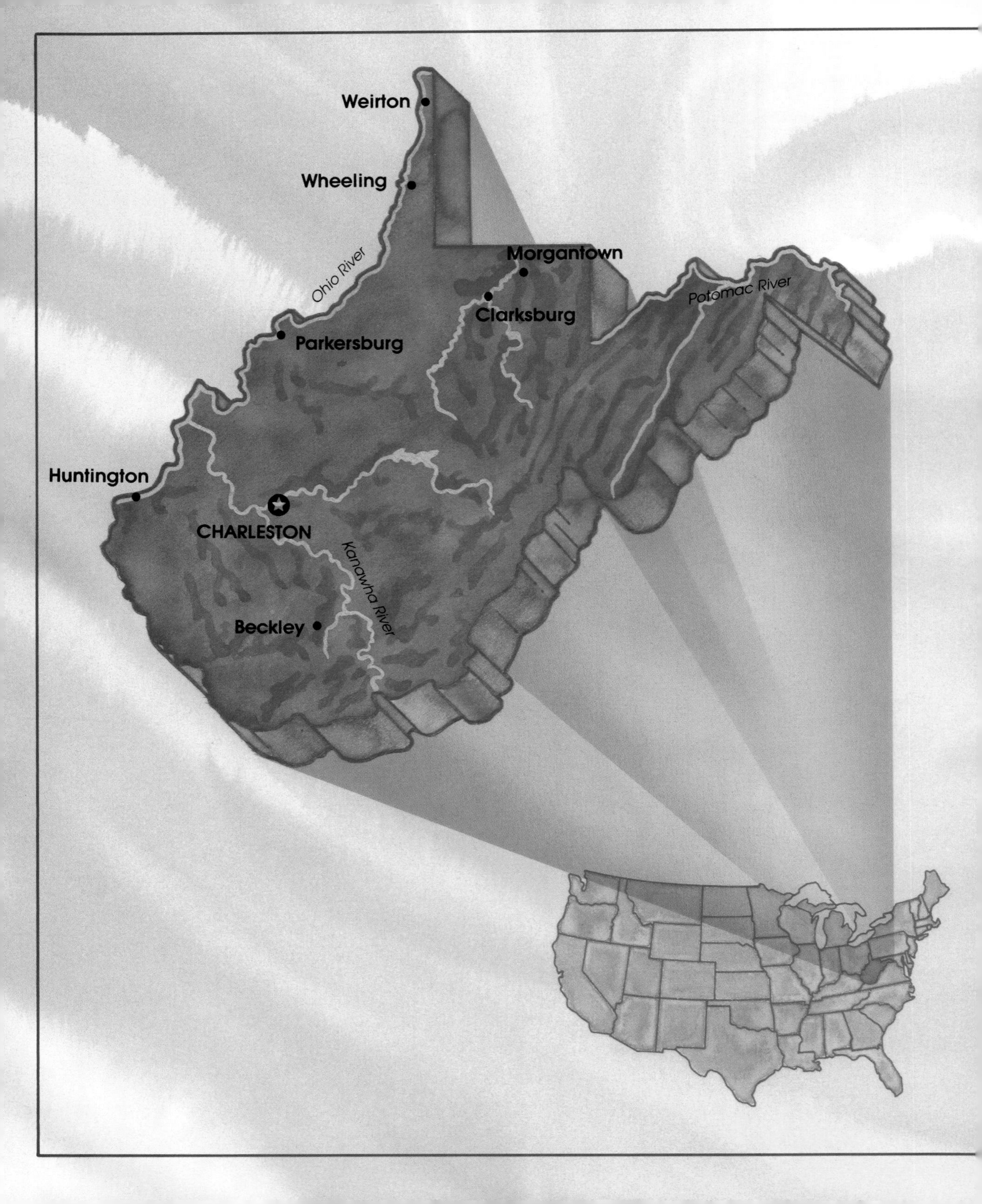

Weirton
Wheeling
Ohio River
Morgantown
Clarksburg
Potomac River
Parkersburg
Huntington
CHARLESTON
Kanawha River
Beckley

CONTENTS

Introduction	7
Mountaineers Are Always Free	8
When the Waters Came Down	20
Gift of the Mountains	22
Making It Work	28
Mining the Rock Coal	32
The Living Museum	36
Make 'Em Dance	40
Mining the Future	42
Important Historical Events in West Virginia	45
West Virginia Almanac	46
Places to Visit/Annual Events	46
Map of West Virginia Counties	47
Index	48

National Park Service photo

Introduction

West Virginia, the Mountaineer State.

"Most of us have roots here, have love here. I buried my father, he died here. My wife—her daddy died here. . ."

West Virginia: coal, mountains, and danger, hard work, good times, and strength of will.

"I've never seen a dull moment since I've lived here. It's been something going off all the time."

West Virginia belongs to its mountains. It's a state almost without level land and with towns you couldn't get to by road until this century. A state carved out of another state, because it was so far from its own homeland. West Virginia is a country state, with towns named Lost City, Falling Spring, White Sulphur Springs, and Strange Creek. It's a state so isolated in parts that you can still find people speaking as they did in England in Shakespeare's time.

West Virginia is a state of the past. It's also a state with its future squarely in front of it.

The grist mill at Babcock State Park.

Stephen J. Shaluta, Jr., Dept. of Commerce, Charleston

Mountaineers Are Always Free

The mountains have determined the history of West Virginia. It was the mountains that drew settlers and it was the mountains that kept them a race apart. The mountains kept them isolated from their home state of Virginia, and, in time, split them into a separate state. The mountains have determined the economy and the way of life ever since.

The first Indians in this mountain place were the Mound Builders. They hunted in the mountains and built great tombs and earthworks near the Ohio River. They built their monuments with little more than baskets and their own strong wills. The Grave Creek Mound built at Moundsville is the largest in the United States.

Centuries after the Mound Builders disappeared, Indians

Seneca Rocks is pictured at left.

Gerald S. Ratliff, Dept. of Commerce, Charleston

Above is Grave Creek Mound in Moundsville.

came to settle in the valleys and hills of West Virginia. But in the mid-1600s Iroquois Indians far to the north went to war against their neighbors. When those Indians proved to be easy victims, they attacked others, and yet others.

The Indians who lived in this region were also attacked. Everyone who lived here was either killed or forced to flee. The mountains of West Virginia were left empty.

Eventually other Indians came back to the land. The Shawnee, Cherokee, Conoy, Delaware, and Susquehanna found excellent hunting among the high mountains. But only the Shawnee settled there. Come winter the others would return to their homes in the north and east.

At times different bands of Indians fought wars over the use of these lands. In the south of West Virginia there was one thing the Indians particularly wanted—salt. It was not easy to come by and it was a valuable commodity for many of the tribes.

However, by the 1500s Englishmen had landed on the coast of Virginia. James I later made a land grant to The London Company in 1606. At that time the boundaries of Virginia went from South Carolina to Pennsylvania, and stretched west indefinitely. All the British land due west officially belonged to the Virginia Colony.

The first European ever to see the region of West Virginia was probably the German explorer, John Lederer. He reached the crest of the Blue Ridge Mountains sometime in 1669. In 1671 Thomas Batts and Robert Fallam also led an expedition into West Virginia territory. They were looking for furs and a way to travel west.

The first real American settler on the land was Morgan Morgan, from Delaware. He settled at Bunker Creek in 1726. Next came a group of German-Americans in 1727. They left Pennsylvania after having religious differences with the colony there. The town they founded was called New Mecklenburg. It's now called Shepherdstown.

Now a wave of settlers began to come over the mountains into West Virginia. They were Scotch-Irish from Northern Ireland, Scots and English. The earliest settlers followed the rivers into the land. They settled along the Ohio River Valley, and in the Greenbrier and New River areas.

Indians were outraged at these settlements on their hunting grounds. They tried to force the settlers out. The raids got worse during the French and Indian War. In 1754 George Washington led an expedition against the Indians, but he wasn't successful. In fact, the following year Indians nearly wiped out a force led by General Edward Braddock.

After the French and Indian War was settled in 1763, King George III issued a decree. There were to be no more settlements west of the Alleghenies unless treaties could be worked out with the Indians.

Some settlers ignored this decree. But it made the colonists work harder to come up with fair solutions. By 1768 agreements were reached with the Cherokee and Iroquois Indians. They would stop hunting in this area and allow settlers to come in. Within the next seven years, about 30,000 people had settled in the region.

Below: costumed tour guides at Prickett's Fort.

Ron Snow, Dept. of Commerce, Charleston

However, no such agreement was reached with the Shawnee. The Shawnee regarded this land as home, and they were not about to let the settlers take over. Shawnee attacks continued for some time after.

West Virginia was frontier country during the Revolutionary War. The British led several raids against settlers in the region, mostly using Indian fighters.

After the Revolution, West Virginia began to develop. The area was rich in minerals and people knew it. In 1794 Peter Tarr built the first iron furnace west of the Alleghenies. In the Kanawha Valley in 1808, salt was being produced from the same areas used by the Indians.

By this time, differences began to appear between the people of western Virginia and eastern Virginia. Western Virginia had been settled by people from the states to the north, such as Pennsylvania and Delaware. Eastern Virginia was primarily plantations and its culture was southern.

The mountains made trade between the two areas difficult. In

Salt production was one of West Virginia's earliest industries. Below: a salt works on the Kanawha River.

Library of Congress

fact, it was difficult to maintain any real contact at all. It was much easier for the people of western Virginia to travel and ship goods west down the Ohio River.

The aristocratic plantation owners of Virginia controlled most of the power in the state. They were not particularly interested in developing the wild mountain regions to the west.

Serious disputes began to arise. Education was a major issue. The well-to-do of eastern Virginia believed that families should pay for their own children's education. They financed private schools. The people of the western counties wanted public schools, so that even poor children could go to school.

Other arguments developed over slavery, taxes, and the way that public money should be spent. The land itself might all have been Virginia, but the east and west had two different ways of life.

Even as the politics simmered, more of West Virginia's resources were being uncovered. Coal was discovered as early as 1742. Natural gas was discovered in 1815. In fact, the western counties were the first place that natural gas was ever used for industry. A salt manufacturer, William Tomkins, used it to power his factory in 1841. Later yet, oil was discovered at Burning Springs in 1860.

But something else happened to change the fate of this part of Virginia. Pro-slavery and abolitionist forces were beginning to affect the country. In 1859, the abolitionist John Brown led a raid against the small town of Harpers Ferry. He planned to capture a munitions arsenal and arm a slave revolt. It didn't work. John Brown and those of his followers who were not killed in the raid were tried and hung for murder and treason. The next year, Abraham Lincoln was elected president. Virginia followed the rest of the South and seceded from the Union.

The western counties would not go along with this. They had their own problems with the aristocrats of the east, and they were not about to follow them into rebellion. The western counties in turn seceded from the state, and formed the Restored Government of Virginia. By April 1862,

West Virginia had its own constitution. West Virginia became the thirty-fifth state on June 20, 1863.

The people of West Virginia were split over the Civil War. About 30,000 men joined the Union Army, but another 8,000 joined the Confederate forces.

Among the most famous West Virginia Confederates was General Stonewall Jackson, who was one of the most brilliant generals of the Civil War. Another famous Confederate was Belle Boyd, an actress. She was tried twice as a Confederate spy, but never convicted.

Once West Virginia seceded, the other Virginians tried to recapture it. As that was not successful, Confederate forces raided the state for food and salt. Salt was not easily found in the Southern states. West Virginia was one of the few sources for it.

Confederate forces also tried repeatedly to destroy the B & O Railroad. This line was a connecting link between Washington, D.C. and the West.

After the Civil War, Virginia petitioned to be reunited with West Virginia, but the new state

Actress Belle Boyd (below) was a spy for the Confederacy during the Civil War.

USDA Forest Service

State Archives, WV Dept. of Culture & History

State Archives, WV Dept. of Culture & History

Railroads made it easier to ship timber and coal out of West Virginia's mountains.

refused. West Virginia had some strong feelings about the Confederacy. After the war anyone who fought for or helped the Confederacy lost his right to vote. Some 15,000 white men had their voting rights taken away. This law was repealed in 1871.

After the Civil War and separation, West Virginia began to develop in its own right. Railroads began to push through the mountain passes. This made it possible to develop the minerals and timberland that were locked away among the mountains.

By the 1880s, the rest of the country was in an industrial boom. Almost all of these industries depended on coal, and West Virginia provided it. From the 1860s through 1920 the mines hired large numbers of West Virginians and European immigrants to work in the mines.

There were regular attempts to unionize the miners. There was little success until the United Mine Workers began to organize in 1890.

The miners were in need of unions. The pay was bad and the work was dangerous. A single mine explosion in 1907 killed 361 miners.

Yet unions were often viewed

Photos: State Archives, WV Dept. of Culture & History

Governor Henry D. Hatfield helped resolve disputes between mine owners and strikers. Below: workers lived in houses owned by the mine.

as very extreme. At that time, striking was considered a radical activity. Everyone in the mine might be fired for it. The company might bring in armed detectives to fight with the workers. It could become an explosive situation.

Miners at Paint Creek and Cabin Creek went out on strike in April, 1912. Fighting broke out and twelve miners and four company guards were killed. Governor William Glasscock sent in the militia. Still the strike went on.

In 1913, a new governor, Henry D. Hatfield proposed a nine hour day and the right to organize. The strikers and mine owners agreed to this and the strike ended in April, 1913.

Soon World War I started overseas, and union activity was quiet while the coal fields helped in the war effort. But after the war was over, the old problems reasserted themselves.

In May, 1920, a new dispute broke out at Metewan. The company locked the miners out of their jobs, and company detec-

tives were brought in to throw miners out of company homes.

Often the company not only owned the mine, it also owned the entire town around the mine. It owned the houses that the miners lived in and the store where they bought their groceries. When the miners challenged the companies, they stood to lose everything.

When the detectives tried to evict the miners' families, city police and miners counterattacked and routed the detectives. More fighting broke out until President Wilson declared martial law and sent in federal troops.

Even worse was a four-day battle that broke out near Blair, West Virginia. Once again federal

State Archives, WV Dept. of Culture & History

Gerald S. Ratliff, Governor's Office of ECD, Charleston

troops had to be sent in. Twenty-two union leaders were tried for treason but found innocent.

However, that incident took the heart out of the union efforts. In 1920, before this defeat, union membership numbered about 45,000. From that point, union membership began to decline. By 1932, there were only about 100 union members left.

After the National Recovery Administration was formed, jobs began opening up around the country. Slowly the factories got under way again. Coal was again in demand. The unions began to regain some of their strength.

Employment hit record levels during World War II, with coal once again fueling the industries. But after the war came a major slump. Factories and cities began to shift to different forms of fuel. Even within the working mines, machinery began to replace miners.

With the drop in jobs, people started to leave West Virginia. It lost seven percent of its population between 1950 and 1960, another six percent between 1960 and 1970. The younger ones went to find new jobs. The older ones remained behind, often living on social security.

Chet Hawes

Congress passed mine safety laws after a 1968 fire at Farmington (above). The left-hand page shows historic and modern-day methods of coal mining.

Even so, the miners who stayed still faced dangerous conditions in the mines. In 1968 an explosion at Farmington killed seventy-eight miners. Congress then passed a group of laws about mine safety. With these were included provisions for black lung, a disease that often affects miners.

Mountains and coal have decided much of West Virginia's history. Now the people of West Virginia have to decide on their future.

When the Waters Came Down

"We evacuated our homes and we spent the night hearing great booms and crashes and hearing cattle bawling and hearing the great rush of water. And not knowing what the situation was, or what had happened to the house or the business or anything."

In late October, 1985, it started to rain in the Blue Ridge Mountains of West Virginia. It rained for eight days solid. The creeks and rivers rose and began to overflow their banks. By November it had turned into the worst flood West Virginia had ever seen. Forty-eight people died, and twenty-two counties were declared disaster areas. Moorefield was just one of the towns affected.

Phoebe Heishman and her family were fortunate in their way.

"The main thing was we knew we were all together and we'd at least survived that way."

A serious flood is much more than just a lot of water. It is a tree trunk crashing through your living room wall. It is a car floating down a river and being crushed by boulders on the shore. It is houses and everything in them being completely ruined. And, a flood is death.

After the flood is a terrible time, a time when everybody has to work together to survive. Phoebe Heishman was the editor of the town's newspaper, the *Moorefield Examiner.* Despite the damage in the office, she managed to get out a special edition of the paper.

"We felt that we owed it to the community to do whatever we could to help people become informed about tetanus shots, where food was available, where water was available. Just basic needs that everybody had at that stage."

After the flood is over, there are even more problems to face. Just finding drinking water becomes difficult. Water might be everywhere, but all of it is contaminated. If you're not careful, you could come down with typhoid or even tetanus from an infected cut.

But the people of West Virginia are tough. It was a setback—a serious setback. It was a shock to see the devastation. Then they started to rebuild.

"Immediately following you had the reaction that 'We're never coming back. Moorefield will never be the same again.'

"Then, as you were able to do things and start cleaning, the whole effort seemed to be. 'We are coming back, we will be coming back bigger and better than ever.'"

The people of Moorefield did return. They did rebuild. And the town is there to tell about it.

Left-hand page: a boy sits exhausted after a day of cleaning up flood damage. Below: houses in Hendricks wrecked by the flood.

Photos: John Warner

4

Ron Snow, Dept. of Commerce, Charleston

Gift of the Mountains

Even as the mountains formed West Virginia's history, they formed West Virginia's economy. For the greatest part of West Virginia's past, the economy meant coal. Coal has its good years and bad. In good times the mines were open and turning out enough coal to power the country. In bad times there were boarded-up mine shafts, empty towns, and people heading north for jobs.

There was a time when coal ran almost everything in this country. Trains were pulled by coal-burning locomotives. Ships burned coal in their engine rooms. People heated their homes with coal.

But now coal is used less and less. Besides, soft coal is what's most common in West Virginia, and it isn't very clean

The Cass Scenic Railroad, a former logging train, hauls tourists to the top of Bald Knob.

Evaws, Dept. of Commerce, Charleston

National Coal Association

to burn. It causes air pollution. In transportation, diesel fuels have become more practical. The demand for coal has dropped. By the early 1960s West Virginia had become one of the poorest states in the Union. It ranked forty-fifth in income, and unemployment was around fifteen percent. It had been dependent on coal for too long.

So the people of West Virginia decided it was time to find some

New industries like chemical manufacturing (above) exist side-by-side with the historically important coal mining industry (left).

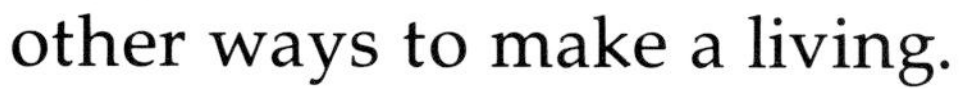

other ways to make a living.

Today mining still accounts for about twenty-seven percent of West Virginia's gross state product. But manufacturing has also become a major West Virginia employer.

In the 1960s the state started offering tax breaks to manufacturers. Factories opened around the state, especially in Weirton. By the 1980s, manufacturing amounted to sixteen percent of the gross state product. The main industries are chemicals, primary metals such as iron and steel, stone, clay and glass products.

One-third of all china sold in the U.S. was made at Homer Laughlin in Newell. Above: firing bowls in glost kiln. Below: hand-finishing sauce boats.

Photos: HLC Company

West Virginia is not a very agricultural state. The land is too hilly to put in field crops. By 1980, only one percent of the popula-

Stephen J. Shaluta, Jr., Dept. of Commerce, Charleston

Gerald S. Ratliff, Dept. of Commerce

Two of the state's small wineries: Little Hungary Winery (left) and Fishers' Ridge Winery (above). At right: apples from the Shenandoah Valley.

tion worked on farms. But even so, in the Shenandoah Valley there is some of the best apple growing country in the world. In fact, West Virginia growers here were the first to develop the Grimes Golden and the Golden Delicious apples.

And service industries account for fifty-four percent of the economy. The largest areas are government, social services, and personal services. Wholesale and retail trade alone account for thirteen percent.

All this has helped to rebuild the economy of West Virginia. By the 1970s West Virginia had climbed to 35th in income among the states. Only seven percent of the people were unemployed.

And people started coming back to West Virginia. When trouble first hit the mining industry, many West Virginians left for Chicago and New York and the automobile factories of Detroit, looking for work. But during the late 1970s and early 1980s, the population began to climb. West Virginia has once again become not only a good place to live but a good place to earn a living.

Photos: WV Dept of Agriculture

Courtesy Darlene McKinley

Instead, Darlene and the other workers of Weirton Steel decided to buy the mill and run it themselves.

"We've always liked each other as neighbors, but now we're linking up arms and—it's a pretty good feeling to know we all felt accountable. Being an employee-owner feels like it's mine. And then if everybody else feels like that it can't do anything but succeed."

Weirton is part of the Rust Belt, a stretch of the Midwest where

Making It Work

"When they had the opportunity to show that they could buy the mill, that we could make Weirton Steel work, that we could do it on our own, that we didn't need a parent company —I think it made everyone feel good."

It was a shock when Darlene McKinley first heard the news that Weirton Steel was closing. Weirton Steel was one of the biggest employers in Weirton. Everybody knew the mill, and everybody knew somebody who worked in it. It would be a disaster for the mill to close. So the town didn't let it happen.

Courtesy Darlene McKinley

factories have been closing down. American industries have been facing stiff competition from foreign imports. But the people of Weirton Mill felt that they had what it took to keep things running and make their mill a working, cooperative effort.

Darlene McKinley is shown at work (left-hand page) and against a view of Weirton Steel (below).

Dept. of Commerce, Charleston

Michael Reagan

Michael Reagan

Lou Fekaris depends on the mill in a different way. He runs a diner near the mill. A lot of his customers work there. So when times got hard at the mill, Lou Fekaris decided to help, too.

"When we first heard that wages would have to be cut, we cut our prices by the same percent as the mill was asked to cut their wages."

Lou's diner stayed full of customers. And Weirton Steel is still in operation. Weirton Steel is more than just a factory in that town. It's been a part of people's lives. It's been a part of their parents' lives, and sometimes their grandparents' before them. Now it's something that belongs to them forever.

"I would look inside the mill and think, 'Oh, my Dad works in there.' I'd like to go in there, but I knew I couldn't. Then, as time went on, I finally did get a job in the mill. It just really felt good, kind of makes chills go over you. Because that's where Dad worked."

At left is the diner owned by Lou Fekaris.

Courtesy Mark McCoy

Mining the Rock Coal

"It was trying times. Hiram was on the day shift. He worked seven to three. We'd always just watch him go and then set there on the porch, me and the one little boy I had then. There was always that worry that he might get hurt. I relied on the Lord more then than ever. Then, it was always a sigh of relief when he came in. Like 'Thank the Lord, another day he was safe.'"

The McCoys are a coal mining family. They have been for generations. It's dangerous work and they know it. It means going down dark narrow tunnels, thousands of feet into a mountain, with the full weight of that mountain hanging over you.

Hiram and Mary McCoy are pictured above. At right is the inside of a coal mine.

And you never know when the weight of that mountain might creak and give way.

But coal mining was the way of life in many parts of West Virginia. Dangerous as it was, it was the job that was handed down, father to son.

Gerald S. Ratliff, Governor's Office of ECD, Charleston

Photos courtesy Mark McCoy

On the left-hand page is Hiram McCoy. Above: Hiram's sons Ken (left) and Mark (right) are shown with their families. Like their father, Ken and Mark work in the mine.

"I didn't really want my boys to start in coal mining. But it's hard to get away from coal mining when you live in the coalfields. I'm one of the fortunate ones, though, that as far as my health is concerned. I've seen a lot younger men that their health is gone."

The worst concern, after mine cave-ins and explosions, was black lung. Black lung is a disease that many miners get. It comes from breathing coal dust for long hours. There's no way to get away from coal dust in a mine shaft. It's everywhere and it gets into everything. A miner can't step over and open a window. He can't step outside when he feels like he needs some fresh air. Instead he has to stay and keep drilling and churning up more coal dust. Eventually, it can kill him.

Michael Reagan

Still, there's a feeling of kinship that develops among coal miners. It's a kinship that comes from hard work, danger, and accomplishment they share. This feeling is often what keeps men working in such dangerous occupations. It can keep workers on the job when simply their wages couldn't do it. And it sets the coal miners apart.

"The miners—they think they're a special breed. And I can identify with that. I think they are."

Ron Snow, Governor's Office of ECD, Charleston

The Living Museum

West Virginia's culture is in the distant past and in the here and now. The high mountains, the deep gullies, and the steep ridges have made much of West Virginia unreachable until this century. Some places were as distant and isolated as when they were first settled by pioneers in the early eighteenth century. In some ways those places have stayed both unreachable and untouched.

In the rest of the country, time moved on—to movies, billboards, and pop music. Those things didn't always make it to the tiny mountain hamlets. There were no phonographs because there was no electricity. And there were no roads to bring in phonographs even if there had been a way to plug them in.

A blacksmith at the Glenville Folk Festival.

Instead the people of the mountains had each other.

The first settlers originally came from Great Britain and Ireland. They brought their folk songs and they brought their language. Because they were so isolated, there were pockets where that language never changed. Even now, Shakespearean scholars from England and America come to West Virginia to record the way the people speak. They believe this is the way the people of Shakespeare's time spoke.

People come to the back hills to hear music for the same reason. Here you can hear songs that date back to seventeenth century Scotland and Ireland, sung very much the same way those songs were sung centuries ago. Modern musicians climb the mountains and record the songs so they won't be lost forever.

Mountain music is played on mountain instruments—the fiddle, the dulcimer, and the mouth harp. They're old instruments for old tunes. Traditional music and handicrafts are celebrated each

At left, Nobel Prize winner Pearl S. Buck is shown with her birthplace in Hillsboro. Right-hand page: Folk culture survives in music (below) and in traditional arts like furniture-making (above).

Photos courtesy Pearl S. Buck Birthplace Foundation Inc.

Gerald S. Ratliff, Governor's Office of ECD, Charleston

year in West Virginia folk art fairs, like the ones at Ripley and Glenville.

Art is to be found in homemade crafts, like quilt making and wood carving. These are often family traditions, passed on from mother to daughter, father to son.

West Virginia has its writers as well. Pearl Buck was an internationally known writer who was born in West Virginia. She wrote such classic novels as *The Good Earth* and *Dragon Seed.* In 1938, Buck won the Nobel Prize for literature.

Margaret Prescott was a more locally known writer writing in the early part of this century. She wrote stories about the mountain people and their ways. In 1920 she won the O. Henry Memorial Prize. She captured some of the feeling of the West Virginia mountains.

There isn't another place in the country like West Virginia. It's a place where some old ways have managed to stay alive.

Ron Snow, Governor's Office of ECD, Charleston

Courtesy Sarah Singleton

Make 'Em Dance

"My father was an old fiddle player from away back. He learned the old-time fashion. That's the only kind I know how to do, because I learned it from him."

Sarah Singleton is a fiddle player. She's one of the old timers. When the Scots and Irish came across from the old country, they brought their fiddles and their jigs and dancing tunes with them. Sarah Singleton plays music that's evolved from that time.

Musical talent is a gift. But not everyone in her family had the gift, or the will to develop it. Sarah did. Her father taught her fiddling and she worked hard at it.

Now Sarah wants to pass it on. But that's not as easy to do these days. People aren't as likely to take time for these things. When you can turn on a radio, making music yourself isn't such an appealing thing.

None of Sarah's kids wanted to learn fiddling. She's hoping one of the grandchildren will want to pick it up. Meanwhile, she's teaching one of the neighbors. Sarah's doing it because she feels it's important to have a fiddler in the community. Sarah feels it's important to pass that skill along.

"She wants to learn real bad. I told her I wanted her to learn so whenever I was gone there'd be somebody else to take my place to play."

Sarah Singleton is working to pass on the skills not only because she wants to keep traditions growing. She's also doing it because fiddle playing is a fine and joyous thing to do. It's fun to play at parties and make people dance and watch them laugh.

"It's just something that gives me a great pleasure to know I can make people happy. Makes you feel good all over."

Sarah Singleton is pictured at right. Above, Sarah gives a neighbor a lesson on the fiddle.

National Park Service

Mining the Future

Just as West Virginia's past is tied to its mountains, so is its future. The mountains define the state. The mountains have kept its culture alive, and the mountains continue to call its people back home.

The mountains will never go away. If airports are to come to West Virginia, they will somehow have to be planted among the mountains. If new factories are to spring up in West Virginia, they will have to bring in their materials and send out their products in spite of the mountains and the twisting passes.

It's not easy to plan around mountains. They contain riches but block radar transmission. Mountains are valuable for themselves as well as what they contain.

There are places where strip mining is tearing the moun-

The town of Hinton is pictured at left.

Gerald S. Ratliff

National Park Service

tains apart. The mining provides jobs for the miners, but people have to decide whether it's worth the price.

The mountains provide beauty and a reason for many people to visit the state. Mountains provide white water and wilderness for rafters and backpackers. Mountains provide quiet in an age where quiet is a precious commodity.

But West Virginia isn't only the mountains. West Virginia is also the people who live in it. And, of course, those people need jobs. West Virginia has to balance those needs.

No matter how many factories and mines go up, the mountains will outlast them all. They'll never go away. They'll always make West Virginia a place worth calling home.

Top of page: rafting the New River Gorge. Left: the mountains that shaped the state's destiny.

Important Historical Events in West Virginia

1640s Iroquois Indians attack other Indians in the region of West Virginia. The area becomes abandoned.

1606 James I of England makes a land grant to The London Company. It includes the region of West Virginia.

1669 John Lederer becomes the first European to reach what is now West Virginia.

1671 Thomas Batts and Robert Fallam lead an expedition into the region.

1726 Morgan Morgan becomes the first American to settle in West Virginia.

1742 Coal is discovered on Coal River by John P. Salley, an explorer.

1754 George Washington leads an unsuccessful raid against Indians during the French and Indian War.

1755 Indians nearly wipe out a force led by General Edward Braddock.

1763 The French and Indian War ends. George III decrees that no settlements are to be founded west of the Alleghenies without treaties with the local Indians.

1768 Treaties are arranged with the Cherokee and Iroquois to allow American settlement of the region.

1777 During the Revolutionary War, Indians, aided by the British, attack western Virginian settlements.

1794 Peter Tarr builds the first iron furnace west of the Alleghenies.

1808 Salt is produced in West Virginia.

1815 Natural gas is discovered near Charleston.

1836 The Baltimore and Ohio Railroad reaches Harpers Ferry. It is the first railroad in the west of Virginia.

1841 William Tomkins is the first to use natural gas to power a factory.

1859 Abolitionist John Brown captures an arsenal at Harpers Ferry. He and his followers are tried and executed that same year.

1860 Oil is discovered at Burning Springs.

1861 Virginia secedes from the Union. The western counties secede from the state. They become the state of West Virginia.

1865 The Civil War ends.

1871 Voting rights are restored to West Virginians who helped the Confederacy.

1890 The United Mine Workers begin to organize coal miners in the state.

1912 Miners at Paint Creek and Cabin Creek go on strike. This is followed by serious fighting. The strike goes on for an entire year.

1920 A miners' strike at Metewan results in more fighting. President Wilson declares martial law and sends in federal troops.

A four day battle breaks out between miners and company guards near Blair. Troops are sent in and twenty union men are tried for treason. They are later acquitted, but the union takes a serious setback.

1968 A mine explosion at Farmington kills seventy-eight miners. Congress responds by passing mine safety laws.

West Virginia Almanac

Nickname. The Mountain State.

Capital. Charleston.

State Bird. Cardinal.

State Flower. Rhododendron.

State Tree. Sugar maple.

State Motto. *Montani Semper Liberi* (Mountaineers are always free).

State Song. The West Virginia Hills; This Is My West Virginia; West Virginia, My Home Sweet Home.

State Abbreviations. W. Va. (traditional); WV (postal).

Statehood. June 20, 1863, the 35th state.

Government. Congress: U.S. senators, 2; U.S. representatives, 4. **State Legislature:** senators, 34; representatives, 100. **Counties:** 55.

Area. 24,181 sq. mi. (62,628 sq. km.), 41st in size among the states.

Greatest Distances. north/south, 237 mi. (381 km.); east/west, 265 mi. (426 km.).

Elevation. Highest: 4,862 ft. (1,482 m) at Spruce Knob in Pendleton County. **Lowest:** 240 ft. (73 m), along the Potomac River in Jefferson County.

Population. 1980 Census: 1,949,644 (12% increase over 1970), 34th among the states. **Density:** 81 persons per sq. mi. (31 persons per sq. km.). **Distribution:** 36% urban, 64% rural. **1970 Census:** 1,744,237.

Economy. Agriculture: cattle, hogs and pigs, broilers, apples, peaches, hay, tobacco, corn, wheat, oats, barley. **Manufacturing:** nonelectric machinery, plastic products, wood products, fabricated metals, chemicals, aluminum, steel. **Mining:** coal, natural gas, petroleum, sand and gravel, cement, crushed stone.

Places to Visit

Berkeley Springs in Morgan County.

Blennerhassett Island, near Parkersburg.

Cass in Pocahontas County.

Charles Town in Jefferson County.

Harpers Ferry National Historic Park.

Monongahela National Forest in eastern West Virginia.

National Radio Astronomy Observatory in Green Bank.

Science and Cultural Center in Charleston.

Seneca Rock in Pendleton County.

Annual Events

White Water Weekend in Petersburg (March-April).

Wildflower Pilgrimage at Blackwater Falls State Park (May).

Mountain State Art and Craft Fair in Ripley (July).

West Virginia State Fair in Lewisburg (August).

Appalachian Arts and Crafts Festival in Beckley (August-September).

West Virginia Water Festival in Hinton (September).

Annual Chrysanthemum Show in Wheeling (November).

West Virginia Counties

INDEX

agriculture, 26
apples, 26
B & O Railroad, 14
Batts, Thomas, 10
black lung, 19, 35
Blair, 17
Boyd, Belle, 14
Braddock, Edward, 11
Brown, John, 13
Buck, Pearl, 39
Bunker Creek, 11
Burning Springs, 13
Cabin Creek, 16
Cherokee Indians, 10, 11
Civil War, 14, 15
coal, 13, 15, 23-24, 32-35
Confederacy, 15
Conoy Indians, 10
culture (of West Virginia), 37-39
Delaware Indians, 10
eastern Virginia, 12-13
economy (of West Virginia), 23-27
employment, 19
Farmington, 19
floods, 20-21
French and Indian War, 11
future (of West Virginia), 42-44
Glasscock, William 16
Harpers Ferry, 13
Hatfield, Henry D., 16
history (of West Virginia), 9-19, 45
Indians, 9-12
Iroquois Indians, 10, 11
Jackson, Stonewall, 14
language, 38
Lederer, John, 10
Lincoln, Abraham, 13
London Company, 10
manufacturing, 25
Metewan, 16
mines, coal, 15-18, 19, 32-35
mining, 25
Morgan, Morgan, 10-11
Mound Builders, 9
Moundsville, 9
mountain music, 38
mountains, 9, 12, 23, 42-44
National Recovery Administration, 19
natural gas, 13
New Mecklenburg, 11
oil, 13
Paint Creek, 16
population, 11, 19, 26, 27
Prescott, Margaret, 39
railroads, 15
Restored Government of Virginia, 13-14
Revolutionary War, 12
Ripley, 39
secession, 13
Shawnee Indians, 10, 12
Shenandoah Valley, 26
Shepherdstown, 11
slavery, 13
statehood, 14
steel, 28-31
Susquehanna Indians, 10
Tomkins, William 13
unions (labor), 15-19
United Mine Workers, 15
Virginia Colony, 10
Washington, George, 11
Weirton, 25, 28-31
western Virginia, 12-13
Wilson, Woodrow, 17
World War I, 16
World War II, 19